Thanksgiving Day

Jessica Morrison

Weigl

Published by Weigl Educational Publishers Limited
6325 10th Street S.E.
Calgary, Alberta
T2H 2Z9

www.weigl.com

Library and Archives Canada Cataloguing in Publication data available upon request.
Fax 403-233-7769 for the attention of the Publishing Records department.

ISBN: 978-1-55388-613-6 (hard cover)
ISBN: 978-1-55388-614-3 (soft cover)

Printed in the United States of America in North Mankato, Minnesota
1 2 3 4 5 6 7 8 9 0 14 13 12 11 10

062010
WEP230610

Editor: Josh Skapin
Design: Terry Paulhus

Weigl acknowledges Getty Images as its primary image supplier for this title.
The National Archives of Canada: page 7 Dreamstime: page 21

We gratefully acknowledge the financial support of the Government of Canada through the Canada Book Fund for our publishing activities.

Contents

What is Thanksgiving?

Thanksgiving is a time to show thanks for peace, family, and good **harvests.** This holiday reminds people across Canada to be thankful for what they have. In Canada, Thanksgiving takes place on the second Monday of October.

Explorers' Thanksgiving

One of the first North American Thanksgiving celebrations was in 1578. English **explorer** Martin Frobisher held a ceremony in Newfoundland. Frobisher did this to celebrate his safe journey to the province. Other explorers also gave thanks for a safe journey. One of these explorers was Samuel de Champlain. He held a celebration called "The Order of Good Cheer."

Official Holiday

In Canada, Thanksgiving became an official holiday in 1879. The holiday was first celebrated on November 6, 1879. Since then, the date has changed many times. In 1931, Canadians began celebrating Thanksgiving on the second Monday of October. Many Canadians have the day off from work and school.

Symbols of Thanksgiving

Foods such as turkey and pumpkin pie are symbols of Thanksgiving. This is because Thanksgiving is celebrated with a special meal. The cornucopia is another symbol of Thanksgiving. It is a large cone filled with many kinds of food. Many people put cornucopias on their table during Thanksgiving dinner.

Family, Friends, and Feast

Many Canadians celebrate Thanksgiving by having a special meal for family and friends. The meal may include a turkey dinner, mashed potatoes, and cranberry sauce. Often, pumpkin pie is served for dessert.

Aboriginal Thanksgiving

Some of the first Thanksgiving celebrations were held by Aboriginal Peoples. First Nations, such as the Blackfoot, would hold a Harvest Ceremony. This ceremony was used to give thanks for a good harvest. The Harvest Ceremony often included dances, games, and races.

14

People in Need

Thanksgiving is a time to help people in need. Many church and community groups make a Thanksgiving dinner. They invite people who are less fortunate to eat the dinner. Some people donate a frozen turkey to the food bank. The turkey is then given to a family in need.

Autumn's Arrival

Thanksgiving is a time to enjoy autumn. Autumn starts in September. Tree leaves change colour in autumn. Most leaves become orange, yellow, or red. These colours are sometimes used to **decorate** the table at Thanksgiving dinner.

18

Jewish Harvest

Jewish Canadians have an autumn harvest festival called Sukkoth. Like Thanksgiving, Sukkoth is a time to celebrate a good harvest. This festival is held in September or October each year. Sukkoth lasts for seven days.

Pumpkinfest

Some places in Canada celebrate autumn with a Pumpkinfest. Pumpkin-carving and **scarecrow**-making contests are often part of Pumpkinfest. Other Pumpkinfest events may include a pumpkin weigh-off. At the weigh-off, people compete to see who has grown the heaviest pumpkin.

Glossary

decorate	explorer
harvests	scarecrow

Index

24

Canal People

Anthony J Pierce

Adam & Charles Black · London

Black's Junior Reference Books

General Editor: R. J. Unstead

Published by A & C Black (Publishers) Ltd, 35 Bedford Row, London WC1R 4JH
ISBN 0-7136-1811-6
Reprinted 1982
© 1978 A & C Black Ltd

Filmset and printed in Great Britain by
BAS Printers Limited, Over Wallop, Hampshire

Fellows, Morton & Clayton
boatyard, Saltley, Birmingham
about 1900

Contents

This boat, on the Thames &
Severn Canal, is being
'bowhauled' by two men.
Boats had been hauled like this
along the rivers for hundreds of
years before the canals were
dug

I   A ribbon of water

A canal is a man-made water channel built to carry
cargo boats. When the canals were built, some
passengers travelled on them but they were mainly
used to transport coal and other goods.

Until the middle of the eighteenth century, Britain
was mainly a farming country and there was little need
to transport vast quantities of goods over long distances.

By the end of the century, Britain was changing into
an industrial country, with towns such as Manchester
and Birmingham growing rapidly. Many people left
the countryside to work in the towns in factories
powered by steam engines which needed many tonnes
of coal to produce the steam. A quicker and cheaper
way of transporting this coal was needed; the
Bridgewater Canal, built in 1761, is thought of as the
beginning of a new transport system, and the start of
'The Canal Era' in Britain.

Packhorses had carried goods
along the roads, but they could
only carry small loads and in
winter the roads were often
impassable

This canal was engineered by a self-taught genius
called James Brindley and was an immediate success.

An aqueduct on the Bridgewater Canal. The price of coal in Manchester was halved because the cost of transport was reduced so much

As a result, Brindley became famous and the demand for canals grew throughout England, but mainly in the North and Midlands. They were specially needed in the areas of the Black Country which provided coal for the steam engines of Birmingham factories.

It was not just coal that the new waterways transported, but food for the increasing town populations, building materials for houses and roads, raw materials to the factories and finished products away from them.

By 1780 the rivers Severn, Mersey and Trent were linked by canal and the framework of over seven thousand kilometres of canal had been laid out.

When James Brindley engineered the Bridgewater Canal, no locks were used; but on his later canals, such as the Staffordshire & Worcestershire and Trent & Mersey, locks had to be used to allow the canal to go up and down hills. These locks were about twenty-two metres long by just over two metres wide. The boats built to go in these locks became known as 'Narrow Boats'.

It is these boats and the people who worked and sometimes lived on them that this book is about.

James Brindley

Taking the census. In 1871 the census recorded 29 500 workers on the waterways, of whom 10 000 worked on the boats

2   The boatman

There are many theories as to where the canal boat people came from. Some people believe the boatmen were gypsies who took to the water but this is almost certainly untrue. Others believe they could have been sailors from coastal ships.

Perhaps originally some boatmen were navvies who, instead of digging the canals, found a less exhausting and maybe better paid life on the boats. As canals spread across the country and trade rapidly expanded, the wages of the boatmen rose above those of many land-based workers. Probably many boatmen were workers from the villages alongside the canals who desired a new way of life.

Wherever they came from, the boatmen quickly established a unique community with a way of life, language and customs of its own. They were sometimes disliked and mistrusted by people on land.

The boatman's wages

The majority of boatmen did not own their boats but worked for a canal carrying company, just as today men drive lorries for transport firms. For this the boatman could receive his wages in several ways.

Many were paid *trip money*, which was a lump sum for a journey or piece of work, instead of receiving a regular wage each week. Today this system is often called *piece work*. Only the captain of the boat actually received money and he then paid his crew. If his wife and family crewed for him, then his wage bill was less than if he had to pay a mate. In 1874 one boatman carried 30 tonnes of coal from Moira in Leicestershire to Oxford, a journey of sixteen days. For this he was paid £5 10s (£5·50), not a lot, even compared with other wages at that time. But some did receive a regular wage.

In the years just before the First World War a company boatman in regular work could expect £1 3s 11d (£1·20) for a forty-eight hour week. In 1919 his wages rose to between £2 16s 10d (£2·84) and £3 4s 6d (£3·23). But as recently as the 1950s the wage for a week's very hard work might be only £6. The next week the boatman might earn £28 and then nothing for several weeks; but he still had to support his wife and family.

On many trips a boatman and his crew had to load and unload the boat as part of their work, although some companies did pay extra for this.

Most of the boats were owned by large carrying companies, including Pickfords, whose lorries you see on the roads today, and the most famous carrying company, Fellows, Morton & Clayton

In winter the canal sometimes froze over for days or even weeks at a time. If a boatman was lucky he received half pay while his boat was frozen in. Some boatmen received nothing

The boatman's working week

Most weeks a boatman rarely knew how many hours he would work. In the days of the horse-drawn boats, a working day depended largely on the horse; it could only be expected to work up to eight hours a day. Company boats had regular stops along the canals where a tired horse could be changed, but a boatman who owned his own animal could not do this. In the early 1920s the internal combustion engine began to replace horses and boatmen would work as many as twelve to fifteen hours a day.

In 1960 a pair of boats on the Grand Union Canal left London at 4.15 am on Thursday December 1st. Working all day, they reached Hatton Bottom Lock in Warwickshire at 7.45 pm, a working day of $15\frac{1}{2}$ hours and a distance of 112 miles and 126 locks. At 6.30 am the following morning, the boats were at work again. On the 9th December the boats worked $12\frac{3}{4}$ hours, and just think how early it gets dark in December! In July the same pair of boats travelled from 5.30 am until 9 pm.

At times the boats could be idle for days, while they waited for orders, or broke down and had to be repaired, or got stuck on the canal bottom. When the boat was idle, the boatman lost money, so no wonder he worked long hours when he could!

Before the horse-drawn boats could begin work, the animals had to be fed, watered and harnessed, adding further to the long day

Breakfast was taken on the move, to save time

A group of Number Ones
moored together, about 1900

The Number Ones

'Number One' is a canal term for a boatman who owned and operated his own boat, instead of working for a carrying company. The Number Ones became the pride of the narrow canals, although there were probably never more than two or three hundred on the canals at any one time. Most canals had their Number Ones, but the greatest number worked in the coal-carrying trade from Warwickshire down the Grand Union Canal to the paper mills at Croxley in Hertfordshire, or on the Oxford Canal carrying coal for domestic use. The boats belonging to the Number Ones could easily be distinguished from the company-owned boats, because they were highly decorated.

On the Grand Junction Canal (which became part of the Grand Union Canal in 1929), the Number Ones generally operated a pair of boats drawn by one animal, while on the Oxford Canal the boats usually worked singly. The Number Ones were very proud of their independence from the carrying companies, proud of their immaculate boats decorated with roses and castles and proud of being able to have their own boats built where and how they wanted.

Retired Number One Mr Joseph Skinner. Note the three polished brass rings on the boat chimney behind him

Joseph Phipkin on his way back empty to the coalfields with his pair of horseboats

Unfortunately, as traffic on the canals declined, it was the Number Ones who suffered first. They could not transport as much or as cheaply as the large companies, nor could they afford a steady reduction in wages.

Unlike the company boatmen, the Number Ones had no regular wage and relied entirely on their work for their living. When the canal iced up they had only their savings to keep them going, and savings did not last long.

By the end of the Second World War few owner-boatmen on the Grand Union Canal could afford to operate on their own and most of them sold out to the larger companies such as the coal-carrying company, Samuel Barlow. On the Oxford Canal, their distinctive boats survived a little longer, the last Number One retiring in 1959. Fortunately, these men and their families took their traditions and way of life into company working with them. Although a minority, the Number Ones played a distinctive role in canal life.

3   The boatman's family

These children posed for a photograph while their parents were preparing the lock for the boats to pass through. The date is about 1914

Some people today live on converted narrow boats moored on a canal. These have many rooms and can be as comfortable as an ordinary house. They can be lit by electricity, have central heating and a refrigerator, in fact all the modern facilities you would expect in a house.

But for the people who lived on working narrow boats, conditions were different from this as they had very little room in their cabin. Forced to sell his cottage and take his wife and family as the crew of his boat, the Victorian boatman was in an unenviable position. The boat was rarely his own and he had no trade union or other organisation to protect him from wage cuts and falling standards of living. On the other hand he did spend his life in the open air and not in a hot noisy factory like many people. However, it was mainly on the canals of the Midlands that people took to living on board their boat.

A boatwoman in her tiny cabin, decorated with lace, lace-plates and family photographs. The range on the left of the picture heated the cabin and was also used for cooking

Steering out of one of the Farmers Bridge locks in Birmingham

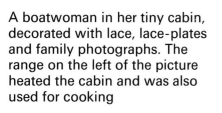

The boatman's wife

It must have been strange for a boatman's wife to leave her small but comfortable cottage on the canal bank for the cabin of a narrow boat, about three metres long by two metres wide and under two metres high.

As space was so limited, the boatman's wife could not take her cottage furniture onto the boat with her, only utensils such as pots and pans, some linen and a few ornaments. The narrow boat cabin was cleverly designed to include all the furniture needed by the family: some items had more than one use. This cabin served the family as lounge, kitchen and bedroom.

The boatman's wife had to run her home as well as or even better than a home on land. Everyday tasks of cooking and cleaning had to be carried out besides looking after the family. In addition the boatwoman was responsible for steering, where she could keep an eye on her children in the cabin.

As she steered, her husband or son would lead the horse or prepare the locks ahead for the boat to pass into when it arrived, thus saving time. To many women, the first year of this new life must have been very strange and hard, but like their husbands they adapted to it and most came to enjoy it.

The family washing, if done on board, would be done in a metal bowl which was used for many other things as well. When the clothes had been washed, usually in spring water, they would be hung out to dry in the hold of the boat.

There was no room for a bath in the cabin of a narrow boat so children sometimes had to wash on the cabin roof

Meals must have sometimes been a problem for the boatwoman because she could rarely 'pop down' to the local shop if she ran out of something. Food was mainly bought at canal-side shops or farms. No doubt on cold days a supply of steaming mugs of tea would be called for. Warming stews formed a part of the family meals and sometimes the meat, whether rabbit, pheasant or perhaps venison, would have been poached by the boatman as the boat passed through a lonely stretch of countryside. In summer when the coal range was not permanently lit, cold meals were common or meals could be cooked on a bankside fire.

A line of washing dries over a cargo of coal

A boatman's children

Some children were born and grew up on the boats. It was far more common however, for the children of boatpeople to be born in a canalside village. Generally, a few days before the baby was due, the boat would moor up at a canal village where the family had relatives. Shortly after the baby had been born, the boat would be on its way again with the baby added to the crew.

A child who lived on a boat rarely met people not connected with boats or the canals, and so lived in the atmosphere of a very large family. Even the children who did not live on the boats, but on the canal bank, shared this way of life.

On the boats children started to help their father as soon as they were strong enough. Their job was often to lead the horse along the towing path or to help at the locks. As the boys grew older they could help even more until they could work a pair of boats on their own. To start with they would do so for their father but later on a son might acquire his own boat.

A child leads the boathorse along the towing path. The metal bowl tied below the horse's neck allows him to eat while walking

A ten-year-old girl steering the boat. From the open hatch, steps lead down into the cabin

A boatman's daughter usually married a boatman, lock keeper or a maintenance man. In this way generations of families became connected with the canals, often spending all their lives on the same canal.

To the children, the boat was their home, playground and often school.

When the boat was moored up, the children often played on the canal bank. The winter months must have been less fun, when children had to stay in the cabin with little room for playing.

In fine weather young children spent much of their time on the cabin roof, commanding a fine view of all that went on around, but where they did not get in the way of the working of the boat. The boat people were very careful about their children's safety and a young child was usually harnessed when sitting on the cabin roof.

Luckily there seem to have been few serious accidents, probably because the children growing up near water learned to be as surefooted as cats.

When the boat was travelling empty between loads, the children could play in the hold. Ropes suspended from the cross planks made superb swings

Boat children's outing in the early 1900s. They don't look as though they are enjoying themselves—but perhaps they were just shy in front of the cameraman

Education

To a boatman time was money and once his boat was loaded or unloaded he would be anxious to be on his way. If his children attended school he would have to wait for them until the end of the school day, a delay he could ill afford. As a result of this, not many boatmen sent their children to school. The 1870 Education Act introduced elementary education but it was not until 1880 that it became compulsory for all young children to attend school. As boatchildren were rarely in one place long, it was difficult to decide where the children should attend school.

When children from the boats did go to school they were often less advanced than other children of the same age, because they did not attend regularly. Because of this they were placed in a lower class and made to feel foolish.

The proud boatpeople hated this and it was a further reason for not going to school. In any case, life on the canal must have been far more fun than in a Victorian schoolroom.

While there was plenty of work on the canals, few children thought of any other job than working on the

The School Board Inspectors tried to make all children attend school

'cut' as the canal was called. They learned the work from an early age and did not really need a school education. But when canal work became scarcer, boatpeople found it hard to find other jobs because they hadn't been to school. Several attempts were made at various times to provide schools for children on the canals. The Incorporated Seamen's and Boatman's Friendly Society, for example, held a school at Worcester Wharf from about 1857, even before education was compulsory. And later the Grand Union Canal Carrying Company opened a school at Bulls Bridge in London.

Although unable to read, a boatman could rarely be short-changed and was also able to understand the tonnage figures on his loading tickets. Those who could read found themselves in considerable demand, particularly when a number of boats congregated together. On these occasions the readers would read aloud from a newspaper, often attracting a fairly large audience.

The boatpeople developed their own form of language, such as 'hackerdock' instead of aqueduct, a corner or a bend being 'a turn'.

This school for canal children was in an old boat on the Grand Union Canal

Boat families spent as much
time as they could outside

Living conditions

In 1873 the difficult living conditions of the people
who spent their lives on the boats of the Midland
canals was brought to the attention of the public by a
Mr George Smith of Leicestershire. He claimed that
on one boat he had been told that three children slept
on a table in front of the fire, two more lay under their
parents' bed and two more in a little cupboard above
the bed. During the Victorian era families were usually
large and as the cabin was the boatman's home there
was bound to be overcrowding.

Certainly such overcrowding existed in the factory
towns of the time and at least the boatchildren had the
advantage of fresh air during the day. Mr Smith also
stated that some of the boat cabins were 'filthy holes
with bugs and vermin creeping up the sides'. Probably
some boat cabins did look like this, as many houses at
the time must have done, but in general the boatpeople
had a reputation for keeping their cabins tidy and
clean. But even where the fore cabin of the boat was
used, or a butty cabin, conditions for some families
would be cramped.

Often a dog became part of the crew, as a friend and guard. The cage on the cabin roof probably holds a pet canary

Overcrowding on the boats was never completely removed but when motor boats came into use a child could sleep on either side of the engine, with possibly a third across the engine. There were of course legal limits to how many people could sleep on a boat. On the Grand Junction Canal the limit for a pair of boats was eight, though six was the average number. Despite these cramped conditions, most boatpeople lived comfortably in their cabins. The Canal Act of 1877 did ensure that the law gave boatpeople some protection from long hours and bad conditions, as factory workers had been given earlier.

Many of the boatmen had a pet on board, frequently a canary. Often a dog became part of the crew, providing a useful guard at night.

On some company boats the boatman had to provide several items of equipment for the boat, such as ropes, chimney or water can. Generally a narrow boat carried about 50 litres of fresh water in two decorated cans on the cabin roof. But canal water was used for many purposes as the water was cleaner than it is now.

Christmas in Wolverhampton 1956

Popular Mission Services

AT THE

BOATMENS' HALL,

—Bridge Street, Birmingham,—

Every Sunday

At 7 p.m.

SPECIAL SINGING.

You are most cordially invited.

Boatmens' Rest Mission,	**Weather Forecast.**
TOP LOCK, WALSALL.	**AN APPEAL.**
	WINTER Cold Winds, Biting Frosts, Rain, Snow, and severe weather generally.
SUNDAY SERVICES:—	
Sunday School, at 10.30 a.m.	**THE POOR**
Afternoon, at 2 p.m.	must need be clothed.
P.S.A., at 3 p.m.	Those old and cast-off garments, &c., for which you have no further use, would
Evening Service, at 6.30 p.m.	shield our poor during the cold weather, and the giver would be happier in the
Monday, at 3 p.m., Women's Meeting.	knowledge that someone was warmer for their gift.
Monday, at 8 p.m.,' Bible Class.	**PARCELS**
Tuesday, at 7.30 p.m., Band of Hope.	will be gratefully accepted, acknowledged and distributed by the—
Thursday, at 8 p.m., Prayer Meeting.	Rev. and Mrs. W. WARD, 26, Gough Road, Edgbaston, Birmingham.

Invitation to a Boatmen's Mission Service

A Salvation Army boat, about 1930. The service was held from the boat while the congregation sat or stood on the canal bank

Religion

Because they had to work on Sunday on some canals, many boatmen had little time to attend church. But some efforts to bring religion to the boatmen were made and a minister would sometimes hold a service by the canal bank where a number of boats had moored. Probably more successful than the churches were Boatmen's Missions established at various points on the canal system. These chapels, though basically places of worship, provided the canal people with a place of relaxation and some education for the children.

The Salvation Army provided not only meeting places for the boatmen but also a boat which became a floating chapel.

Relations with people on the bank

To many people on the bank, boatpeople appeared unfriendly, quaint, illiterate or even troublesome. Canal people kept to themselves and led rather isolated lives, so other people were often suspicious of them. But of course boatpeople did mix with people on the land at times.

Many boatmen had once worked on the land and had non-boating relatives. On some canals, the farmers whose land was next to the canal used it to carry their produce and therefore had a working relationship with the boatmen.

Stourport, about 1790. This town grew up at the point where the Staffordshire & Worcestershire Canal entered the River Severn. Almost all the townspeople depended on the canal for their living

4   Other canal people

The proprietors

After the success of the Bridgewater Canal, one of the earliest canals to be built was the Trent & Mersey. One of the men who wanted this canal built was Josiah Wedgwood, founder of the famous pottery firm. He believed that a canal would enable him to get the clay needed in his factory, near Stoke-on-Trent, from Liverpool more easily and quickly than by road. Also he thought that there would be few breakages if the finished pottery was transported from the factory by boat. Josiah and some other businessmen asked Brindley to survey a route which would eventually run from the Duke of Bridgewater's canal at a village called Preston-on-the-Hill near Liverpool, through the Potteries to join the River Trent near Derby. At the same time a canal was planned to connect the Trent & Mersey with the River Severn. This was called the Staffordshire & Worcestershire Canal.

The route of a canal is discussed by the promoters. Such discussions could be heated because some landowners or towns stood to lose or gain from the choice of route

The two sides of a toll token for the Bridgewater Canal

These men and others like them became known as canal promoters. Satisfied with Brindley's proposals, the promoters called a meeting of all people interested in lending money to pay for the building of the new canal. There was no shortage of people who thought that the canal was a good idea. They readily bought shares and therefore became its proprietors. By buying shares, usually worth £100 each, people were lending money to the canal company. So great was the enthusiasm for canal building that shares bought for £100 one day could be worth £200 only a day later.

Many proprietors were rich landowners or businessmen but some less wealthy people also bought shares as they became caught up in the enthusiasm for the new form of transport. Of course, all shareholders hoped that the canal would be a success and carry a lot of traffic because the more traffic the canal carried, the more money the canal company would receive in tolls. These were the charges made for carrying goods on the canal and they varied with the type of material carried.

On some canals shareholders made a lot of money, but on others they received very little and lost the money they had originally lent.

Canal engineers

In the life of a canal the engineer was an important person. Some engineers, like Brindley or Thomas Telford, became famous while other men worked on only one canal and were never heard of again.

Naturally the proprietors liked to have a well-known engineer. As a result, some engineers found themselves responsible for several canals at the same time. It was impossible for them actually to supervise the building of each canal, as Brindley had done on the Bridge-water, so they would appoint a resident engineer to stay on one canal and be responsible to the main engineer who rode from one site to another. He naturally took great care in choosing the resident engineer and would sometimes appoint one of his own pupils.

One of the engineer's first tasks was to decide the line that the waterway would take through the country-side. This plan had to be drawn so that people could see where the canal was to go and it also needed to be sent to Parliament. Before any canal could be built, an Act of Parliament had to be passed. While many landowners welcomed the new canals, some did not like them at all and used their influence to oppose the Act of Parliament.

Engineers watch the water flowing into the Manchester Ship Canal. There are scarcely any pictures of the narrow canals being built, so we have to rely on these later photographs of this much wider and deeper canal

Thomas Telford 1757–1834, a famous engineer

Most landowners welcomed the canal passing through their land, either because they had shares in the canal or because the company had said that goods from their farms or factories could travel free.

When Parliament had granted permission, contractors had to be found to organise the actual digging and building of the waterway. The contractors who built the canals were not like the huge construction companies that build motorways today. They were men who had often found work re-surfacing turnpike roads or building houses in their locality.

Many went bankrupt doing canal work; others just failed to finish their stretch of canal and had to be replaced by another contractor, but most did a satisfactory job.

Normally a contractor would be employed by the canal company to build a length of the canal. Thomas Telford, for example, insisted that a contractor had one difficult length and one easy one. Once employed, the contractor had to find men to do the work for him. These men became known as 'the navigators', later shortened to the word *navvies*, because they worked on inland navigations.

Navvies' tools

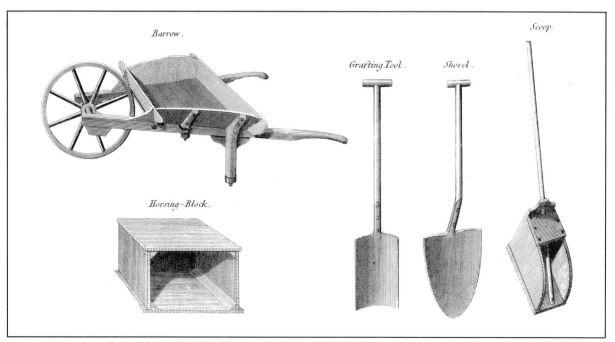

The navvies

The navvies were employed to dig or 'cut' the channel of the canal while special tradesmen were hired to build bridges, tunnels and locks. Sometimes these men became the canal maintenance men once the canal was finished.

The navvies generally moved around the countryside from one canal to another in gangs. Some canal engineers won the respect and loyalty of the navvies by treating them fairly, but other engineers found that all their navvies would leave them overnight if they discovered better wages being paid on a different canal.

The wages received by the navvies varied from area to area. In the Midlands plenty of men moved from working in the collieries and ironworks to become navvies and it was not too difficult for a contractor to build up his gang. Finding navvies for rural areas could be more difficult. Many agricultural workers found the strict discipline and rough living conditions of a navvy's life too demanding and not even the promise of high wages could entice them to the work.

As navvies moved about the country they often left behind them a reputation for drunkenness and rioting.

Navvies taking a meal break, Manchester Ship Canal, 1887. Even at this time, much of the digging was done with a pick and shovel, and the earth was moved away by wheelbarrow

A navvies' outfitter selling clothes, about 1890

At the beginning of the nineteenth century, there was a shortage of coins in England. Banks, fearing robbery, did not keep large amounts of money and not enough coins had been minted anyway. The navvies received their wages weekly and, as a result of the coinage shortage, they sometimes found there was no money to pay them. No wonder riots broke out in some villages!

During the time canals were being built, the price of food and materials needed to build the canal rose. This meant the contractor had to reduce the amount he spent on his work. One of the first things he did was to cut the wages of the navvies. There was little the navvies could do about this since they had no Union to protect them.

Tommy shops

Because of the shortage of money for wages, some canal companies operated *tommy shops*. A navvy would receive all his wages in tokens which could only be spent at the tommy shop. Since the canal company owned the shop, it could obviously fix the prices to make a profit out of its own workmen.

A navvy's life

The life of a navvy was dangerous and accidents regularly happened. Tunnelling was highly dangerous; many navvies were killed by rock or earth falls or by gunpowder explosions going wrong. On the ordinary digging of the canal some men were buried alive when excavating an embankment. Other men could be badly injured or killed if a wheelbarrow slipped while being pulled up a slope. An accident rate of one or two deaths for every mile of canal was common.

In addition to these risks the conditions in which the navvies lived and worked meant they were more likely to catch diseases than other workers. Some canal companies paid a fee to local hospitals to care for injured workers or for a doctor to visit the work site. The religious group known as the Quakers, took care of many navvies and provided a great deal of medical attention.

Most navvies were probably unable to read or write, but they did pay for the upkeep of a kind of news service: disabled navvies who wandered from one canal to another keeping the men informed of both news and wages.

Tunnelling was dangerous work. This 900 metre long tunnel was dug for the Regent's Canal, 1819

Wreckage after an explosion on the Regent's Canal, near London Zoo, 1874

The maintenance men

Once built, a canal had to be kept open for boats to use it twenty-four hours a day if necessary. This was the job of the maintenance men employed by the canal company. This team included bricklayers, stone-masons, blacksmiths, carpenters, labourers, lock-keepers and even a saddler in days when horses towed the boats.

Most canal companies built large maintenance work-shops alongside the canal, in which lock gates could be made, boats repaired and the tools for the men both made and repaired.

A stoppage on the canal, when boats could not move, was something to be avoided in the working days. Serious work such as replacing the bottom gates of a lock was usually carried out at holiday times when few boats would be working. Less serious repairs could be carried on between boats.

Repairing a canal tunnel, using an airshaft to gain access

The work of the maintenance men was varied. The blacksmith not only shod horses but mended tools and made iron parts for the locks. The carpenter would make wheelbarrows, ladders, windows and doors for canal cottages and eventually, after years of practice, lock gates.

Just as the boatmen worked in families on the cut so too did many maintenance men, a father often handing on his job to his son. At the age of about 13 years a boy joined the maintenance gang. Early in the

Tinsmiths at work in a maintenance workshop, Ellesmere Port, 1892

morning the young apprentice would sweep out the boat's cabin and have a cup of tea ready for the men when they arrived. In return for this, and for preparing their tools, the men would teach the boy their skills and provided him with his own set of tools.

Dredging is a vital part of any maintenance work. If the canal channel is not kept clear of silt and rubbish then boats have great difficulty in using the canal and in the days of working boats this meant a loss of money.

The lock-keeper is not only responsible for looking after his flight of locks but also, with the lengthsman, for repairing the towpaths. One of the main jobs of these two men is to see that water levels do not get too high in a canal and cause flooding. Sometimes the lock-keeper may be called out during the night to control the level by releasing water through sluices, often into a nearby river or stream.

Rebuilding a lock, 1900

Boatbuilder's yard on a canal bank, 1908

5   Some boats on a canal

The boats we shall look at in this chapter are mainly those that traded on the narrow canals.

Originally most canal traffic was local, the boats carrying goods for short distances. When the Trent & Mersey Canal opened in 1777, a through route between Manchester and the Midlands was created. This meant that new faster boats had to be built to transport goods over longer distances. The boats built for this were the Narrow Boats, and until the 1960s these boats could be seen all over the canal system carrying many kinds of cargo such as coal, grain, flour, timber or clay. From the early days of canals until the 1920s and even later, they were drawn by a horse, donkey or mule. Later, the boats had engines.

Narrow boats

Sometimes the boats have been called Long Boats because of their size. Another name given to them is Monkey Boat. Originally the boats had no cabin, as the men working them returned home most nights, but longer journeys meant that a cabin was needed. Thomas Monk is thought to have been the first man to fit a living cabin on the stern of a canal boat, which is why they are called Monkey Boats.

Boatbuilding

At one time there were many boatbuilders' yards on canal banks. Some of the most popular firms were at Northwich, in Cheshire, the village of Braunston in Northamptonshire, Rickmansworth in Hertfordshire and Uxbridge in Middlesex. Today a few yards remain but very few now build working Narrow Boats; instead, they build and repair pleasure boats and maintain the few Narrow Boats that are still working.

Most of the boatyards were owned and run by a family who employed perhaps six to ten men, some of them being brothers, uncles and cousins. Each man was skilled in his own craft, as boatbuilder, blacksmith, carpenter or painter. Often the boatyard owner decorated the boat himself, taking a great pride in the work.

Men working for small firms and building the boats by hand did not produce large numbers of boats although some Black Country yards produced up to forty Day Boats a week. No two boats were ever exactly alike; there may have been only small differences, perhaps in the painting, but each one was unique.

Most boats were built in the open, but here one is being constructed under cover. The boatbuilder rarely had a set of plans to work from: instead, he kept much of the knowledge in his head, or had a few sketches in a notebook

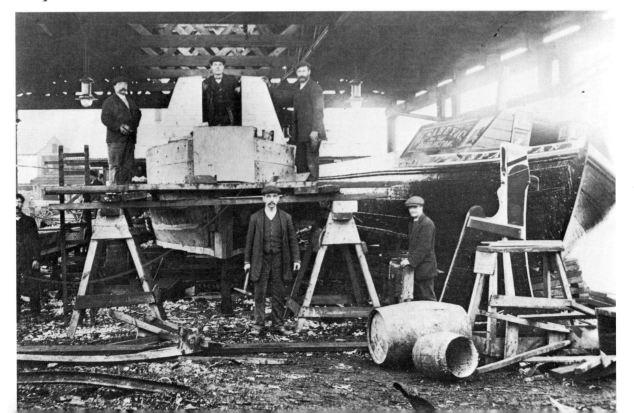

Originally all Narrow Boats were built of wood; seasoned oak made up the side planks, because of its strength, while the bottom was made of elm. This was very slow to rot if kept constantly under water.

One of the most beautiful parts of a Narrow Boat is the fore end, where the timbers are curved.

The builder used the natural curve of the wood for the fore end, and would look for suitable branches of trees. When the tree was felled he would buy it. When wood had to be shaped for use in other parts of the boat, this was done by steaming it in a large box so that it could be bent.

The last Narrow Boat made entirely of wood was built in 1958 but by that date most boats had been built of wood and steel, or iron, or all steel, especially boats with an engine.

A pair of working narrow boats at Cosgrove, near Wolverton

Once the hull had been shaped, the cabin was built and decorated, sometimes before launching, sometimes afterwards. The hull of the boat had to be watertight.

All the joints between the planks of the hull had to be filled with strands of *oakum*, a rope made waterproof, which was hammered into the joint by hand. This was known as *caulking*.

The joint would then be given a coat of pitch mixed with tar and finally the whole hull was painted. Inside the hull, men applied a coating of *chalico*, a mixture of horse dung, cow hair and tar which helped to seal the joints and make the hull waterproof. On top of this a covering of brown paper or oiled felt was placed, followed by a lining of thin sheets of oak. Not only did this help in waterproofing but it also prevented the strands of oakum being pushed through from the other side.

Eventually the time for launching came. The boats were often launched sideways down greased planks. In the 1920s the cost of a new boat was around £220, but by the early 1950s this had risen to about £1500.

The life of a Narrow Boat depended, of course, on how well it was looked after. Each year most boats were checked over but were *docked* every three years or so. This meant they returned to a boatyard, often the one at which they had been built, to be given a thorough check.

Boats were usually launched sideways. This Fellows, Morton & Clayton wide boat is being launched in the 1930s

Caulking the seams with oakum

Factories were often built on canal banks for easy loading and unloading. In this picture, beer is being loaded into the boats while empty casks are taken back to the brewery

Trade

The main cargo was coal to supply firstly steam engines and later boilers of factories. Many of these factories were on the canal bank but those that were further away received their coal by horse and cart and later by lorries, often owned by the canal carrying companies.

On the Trent & Mersey Canal all types of cargo needed for the pottery trade around Stoke-on-Trent arrived by boat and most of the pottery left the factory in the same way. So successful was canal carrying, compared to road transport, that many factories were built alongside canals for easy loading and unloading from the boats. Some factories even had covered loading areas.

Some boatmen worked on regular runs carrying the same cargo on every trip, while others worked all over the canal network finding loads to carry from one place to another. One day the boat might be loaded with wheat, the next day with coal or tinned food. Large amounts of salt went via the Worcester & Birmingham Canal to Worcester or Gloucester.

On the journey back to Birmingham, the boat often carried hay, straw, beans, barley or potatoes collected from farmers' wharves along the canal.

Flour, cheese, sugar, cocoa beans, tea, milk, butter, sand and manure were also carried in the holds of Narrow Boats; in fact, nearly all the things that are carried by lorry today. Some Narrow Boats were made especially for certain types of goods: boats carrying tea, for example, had their holds lined with metal to prevent dampness and their hatches locked to prevent theft.

Most of the canal boats belonged at first to a carrying company and not to the canal company itself. Some of these companies were large firms with boats working over much of the canal system. Probably the best known of these was Fellows, Morton & Clayton. Other companies only had a few boats, perhaps working in one area. The companies advertised the goods they carried and the charges they made.

Where a customer wanted to send goods to a place not served by his local canal carrying firm, the goods would cover part of the journey in one boat and then be transferred to another.

A boat laden with crates of crockery passing Staffordshire 'bottle kilns' on its way to Liverpool docks, 1942

Fresh milk on its way to a Cadbury factory, to make milk chocolate

Fly boats

These boats were built like the Narrow Boats but were both lighter and shorter, about nineteen metres long. Although they could not carry as much cargo as the other boats, they travelled much faster. Fly Boats worked day and night to provide the fastest possible carrying service. Travelling at about six kilometres per hour when fully loaded, they could carry perishable goods, such as food, far more quickly than a normal craft travelling at two or three kilometres per hour.

To keep up their speed the Fly Boats changed horses at frequent intervals along the route and ran to a regular timetable. Normally the crew of a Fly Boat was made up of four men, double the usual Narrow Boat crew. One man steered, while two men worked the boat through the locks; the fourth man usually slept.

Market boats

Market boats worked over short distances and their crew returned home each evening. On the Grand Union Canal, for example, market boats picked up fruit and vegetables from the countryside around London and took them each morning into market. Milk in many parts of the country was brought into towns in this way. Other boats collected farm produce from farms along the canal.

Unloading a market boat

Packet boats

Canal boats mainly carried cargo, but some of them also carried passengers. Almost from the opening of his canal, the Duke of Bridgewater operated passenger boats. Originally these boats had two classes of accommodation, first and second, but although only the first class had carpeted floors, all the travellers could buy tea and cakes. By 1770, boats carrying 120 passengers in three classes were running to a timetable.

One of the Duke's boats, named *The Duchess Countess*, carried a sharpened 'S' shaped knife at the front. Packet boats were allowed to overtake all other craft and in horse-drawn days, if a slower boat did not let go its towing rope, so that the Packet boat could pass, then the knife would cut the rope, leaving the boat no longer attached to its horse.

During the reign of Queen Victoria, canals became popular for day trips, especially for children from Sunday Schools. Queen Victoria thought highly of the boatmen and their work and in 1851 she paid a visit to the Bridgewater Canal.

'Joey' boats

The usual name of these boats which worked mainly on the Birmingham Canal Navigations was a Day Boat.

Packet boat trips were so popular that sometimes they became very overcrowded. This boat carried passengers along the Grand Junction canal from Paddington to Uxbridge, 1801

'Joey boats' or 'day boats' on the Birmingham Canal Navigations in 1953

The box-like BCN Day Boat could be steered from either end; it had no living cabin. The men who worked these boats normally returned home each night, since they seldom worked far from their home.

The life of a Day Boatman, even though he could go home at night, was in some ways harder than his long distance companion. On the Birmingham Canal Navigations it is estimated that at one time there were 2000 wharves serving factories and the boatman had to know every one of them, as well as all the small canal arms on which they stood. The crew of a Joey consisted of one man and a mate, often a boy who might work one day and disappear the next. Not only did their work consist of steering the boat, but of loading and unloading the forty tonnes of coal, iron or ashes the boat usually carried. And the boatman had to tow his boat through the locks by hand.

During the time of the horse-drawn boats and even up to the late 1930s on the Birmingham Canal Navigations, thousands of horses would be at work on the canals. One of the carrying jobs of some boatmen was to collect the horse manure and remove it to farms in the country.

Icebreakers

Of the many other types of boats on the canals one of the most important was the Icebreaker. A great fear of all boatmen was that the canal would freeze up in winter. With wooden boats they dared not try to break thick ice as this would smash a hole in their hull.

Once the ice had become thick enough to stop boats moving, a special boat came into use. This boat had a rail along the middle; several men clung to the rail and rocked the boat from side to side while a team of horses, sometimes twenty or more, pulled the boat. If this broke up the ice, the Narrow Boats followed the Icebreaker through the channel. Sometimes, however, the ice was too thick and the boats remained frozen in for weeks at a time. This happened in 1947 when many boatmen were left stranded, often out in the country far from a village. Not until a thaw came could the Icebreaker get through.

A horse-drawn ice-breaker at work in 1934. The men held the rail in the centre and rocked the boat from side to side, breaking the ice, while the horses pulled the craft forward

6   Propulsion

Manpower

Until boats powered by steam or diesel engines came into use on the canals, nearly all boats were pulled by a horse, donkey or mule, although often, especially at locks, boats had to be bowhauled.

Few tunnels had towpaths inside them because they were too costly to build and therefore it was at canal tunnels that manpower was mostly used, since the horse could not pull the boat through the tunnel without a towpath.

Leggers

When a Narrow Boat arrived at a tunnel, the horse would be unhitched and led over the top of the tunnel by the boatman's mate or his children. The pathways that the horses took can still be traced at some tunnels such as Blisworth on the Grand Union Canal. This walk provided a rest for the horse and a chance for some fun for the children.

All Narrow Boats working on canals with tunnels carried a pair of planks, or *wings* as they were

Although mainly a thing of the past, bow-hauling is occasionally used even now. This photograph was taken in 1972

Legging. The narrow planks on which the men lie are called wings

sometimes called. These would be laid on the fore end of the boat before it entered a tunnel. A man then lay on his back on each plank, sometimes putting an old coat down first to provide some comfort. The men would then 'walk' along the tunnel walls to propel the boat through. Getting the boat moving was the hardest part of their job but in a dark wet tunnel no part can have been easy.

Since the width of tunnels varied, the boats had to carry two pairs of wings, a short pair and a long pair.

In very narrow tunnels, no wings were necessary. It took about 2¼ hours to leg a boat through this tunnel

The men who did this work were known as *leggers* and they worked for the canal company. They usually spent their time waiting for boats in a small brick hut provided for them at either end of the tunnel. Some of these huts can still be seen at tunnel entrances today.

The leggers were paid a sum of money for each boat they legged through. This varied according to the length of the tunnel and the time it took them for the journey. In the Standedge Tunnel on the Huddersfield Narrow Canal, for example, two hours was a normal time to leg a boat through the 5210 metres of low tunnel. If the boat carried under 12 tonnes of cargo the rate of pay was 1s (5p); for over 12 tonnes, 1/6d (7½p) was paid. Even compared to other people's wages at the time, this was very poor pay.

Conditions in the tunnels could be dangerous, with a chance that part of the roof might collapse. Also, most tunnels had water constantly dripping from the roof onto the face and clothes of the leggers.

Some boatmen chose to leg their boats through tunnels themselves or would employ only one legger. This was cheaper, for if the boatman employed two leggers he had to pay for the second one out of his own wages. In very low tunnels and with an empty boat the boatman could lie on the roof of his cabin and walk along the tunnel roof.

On the Worcester & Birmingham Canal the leggers at Tardebigge Tunnel spent much of their waiting time at a public house, close to one end of the tunnel. Perhaps it is not surprising, as legging must have been thirsty work! Unfortunately, while waiting for boats they sometimes drank too much and some leggers were drowned. The public house had to be closed down.

Legging was a slow job and on busy canals queues of boats soon built up waiting to go through. To overcome this, steam tugs came into use on many canals, towing a number of boats behind them. This meant that the leggers became redundant and they finally disappeared when the vast majority of Narrow Boats were motorised. The few horse boats left then relied on a tow from a passing motor boat.

Legging was thirsty work and some leggers spent rather too much time in the pub at the end of the tunnel

A steamtug towing a boat through Braunston Tunnel. The horses on the towpath have to come over the top of the hill, and are waiting for their boats to emerge

Animal power

The horses, donkeys and mules that pulled the canal boats were known to the boatmen just as 'animals' or, as they pronounced it, 'hanimals'.

Normally a horse would pull a single boat with one member of the boat's crew leading it. Once trained for their work the animals quickly learned where to stop at a lock so that the boat did not run into the gate and how to keep the boat travelling smoothly. The hardest part of the work for a boat horse was to get the boat moving, especially when loaded. Once he had done this, a good horse could pull up to fifty tonnes without strain, often working from dawn to dusk, but not non-stop.

Most canal horses were well treated by the boatmen, especially those of the long distance men. To most men, the horse was their next consideration after looking after their family. Many canal carrying companies expected the boatman to buy his own horse. In addition to this the boatmen had to provide the harness and food. To work hard all day, the animal needed regular grooming and feeding. Enough food for a trip would be carried in the boat and the horse was fed during the day with the boat still moving, though he was allowed to slow down to eat.

Two horses about to be led over the Braunston Tunnel

Boat horses were fed from a special metal bowl and this had a handle on either side so it could be hung from the harness. Some boatmen, notably the Number Ones, decorated the bowls with roses and castles but due to the rough treatment they received, this soon wore off and many boatmen did not bother at all.

The harness of some boat horses was decorated with polished brasses but this was not very common. More often they had brightly painted wooden bobbins on the trace ropes. The bobbins prevented the ropes chaffing the horse's skin while he was working.

A healthy horse was essential to a boatman and some men would go without food themselves rather than see their horse go hungry. Many boatmen showed a great pride in their horses, keeping them well groomed and exhibiting them at horse fairs, as on the Trent & Mersey Canal. These horse fairs were great occasions, with a parade through the town before judging took place. On the day of the fair the horses would be decorated in an array of brass and well-polished leather.

Decorated harness, with polished brasses, for a special outing on the Monmouthshire Canal

Left: crocheted earflaps were sometimes worn by the horses as a protection against flies. Right: one of a pair of donkeys, pulling a narrow boat, about 1905

In the summer when horses could suffer from the torments of flies and insects, the boatwomen often crocheted special earcaps for the horses to keep away the pests.

On some canals, most notably the Worcester & Birmingham, donkeys rather than horses pulled the majority of the Narrow Boats, though horses were used as well. Normally a pair of donkeys worked together to pull a single boat. This was fine as long as they had been trained together and had become friendly. If they had not, then trouble quickly arose.

On one occasion a young lad working with his father had to lead a pair of donkeys over Tardebigge Tunnel while the boat was taken through. Released from pulling the boat the two animals, who had not previously worked together, galloped away from each other with the lad in pursuit. By the time he caught them, the boat and his father had been waiting at the end of the tunnel for two hours and neither the lad nor the donkeys were popular.

Donkeys were never as widely used on the canals as horses, possibly because they had to work in pairs and were a little slower than a horse. On the other hand they ate virtually anything and cost little to buy.

Steam power

After the introduction of steam engines in factories, it was not long before experiments were made with steam-powered boats.

Steam boats had both advantages and disadvantages over the horse boats. The main disadvantage was that, because of the amount of room needed for the boiler and engine, the boat could not carry as much cargo as the horse boat. However, the great power of the new craft enabled it to tow another boat behind it, known as 'The Butty'. This made up for the loss of cargo space in the boat itself. Unlike the horse, which needed to rest, the steam boat could operate 24 hours a day if necessary and they often did. To allow them to do this, the steamers carried a crew of four, two working at a time. One man stoked the boiler and looked after the engine, one steered and the other two rested. A family normally lived in the butty and it was their job to work the locks. Working day and night, the journey from Brentford in London to Birmingham of about 220 kilometres and 151 locks could be managed in 52 hours.

Steam boats became the pride of Fellows Morton and Clayton who operated them from the early 1900s and kept them in constant use.

Steam tug towing a number of wide barges down the Grand Union Canal at Kensal Green gas works in 1931 —just before the steam tugs were replaced by motor vessels

As soon as the steamer arrived at the company's wharf it would be unloaded and loaded again for a return journey so that the boat was not kept idle. If the cargo in the butty was not being unloaded at the same place as that in the steamer, it would be taken to its destination by horse, the steamer meanwhile having collected another loaded butty. The coke-burning steamers were successful as long as they kept moving and so they generally used main canal routes such as between London and Birmingham, Leicester or Nottingham.

Not only did steam find a use in Narrow Boats, it also speeded up traffic at tunnels. As early as 1875, steam tugs had replaced leggers in Tardebigge Tunnel, towing up to eight boats at a time. The tug service operated every two hours, starting in the summer at 4 in the morning and running until 8 at night or longer.

At first, smoke from the engine made life for the tug crew and the boatmen very unpleasant, until the tug men realised that if they built up a good head of steam before entering the tunnel and had a clean fire, they could get through the tunnel without smoke. Certainly the tugs were kept busy pulling between 50 and 75 boats a day through, just before World War One.

A Fellows, Morton & Clayton steam narrow boat: this boat towed a single 'butty'

A diesel boat, 1948. The steady beat of the diesel replaced the clip-clop of the horses hooves

Diesel power

Early in the twentieth century various experiments took place to find other types of boat engines that did not take up as much cargo space as the steam engine and needed a less bulky fuel.

The engine that became most popular to do this was the Bolinder, a type of diesel, first fitted in a Narrow Boat about 1906. Although a bit noisier than the almost silent steam engine, the Bolinder was as efficient but needed only one crew for both boats. This obviously saved men's wages, while more cargo could be carried.

With the success of this engine, others soon followed and motor boats quickly became popular with the canal carriers.

By the 1940s, horse-drawn boats had become a rarity on the canal although some of the Number Ones, mainly using the Coventry and Oxford canals, carried on using horses. And even today, horse-drawn boats are not quite extinct.

Some boats used wind power. Narrow boats using sails were extremely rare, but the keels of some northern waterways and wherries of Norfolk relied on the wind for their movement.

A two cylinder steam launch engine

The stern of a narrow boat. Notice the magnificent knotting decorations on the rudder post—see page 54

Roses decorate this dipper, and a castle scene appears on the wooden block above

7 Canal art and folklore

Narrow boat decoration

No one really knows how the Narrow Boats came to be painted with the geometric patterns and roses and castles which have become known as the traditional style.

The earliest boat decoration was probably very simple lettering on the side of the boat showing the name of the boat owner. Roses and castles did not begin to appear until the boatmen took their families to live on the boats with them. Just as the boatman's wife had been proud of her cottage on the canal bank, she wanted her new home to be attractive. Bright painting on the outside of the boat was one way of showing this pride.

Why roses and castles were chosen for the decoration is really a mystery. But many everyday things of the early nineteenth century, such as teapots or dials of the popular grandfather clocks, were painted with flowers or landscape scenes. As people moved onto the canal boats it was natural that the type of painting they knew and had in their homes should move with them. And so the landscape scenes appeared on the boats. Later, as boatpeople developed their own way of life, a certain style of painting also developed, the roses looking not like real roses and the castles like fairy castles.

Not all Narrow Boats were highly decorated. Many of them belonged to canal carrying companies and simply had geometric patterns on the fore end of the boat or scroll work around the owner's name on the cabin sides.

Originally the main colours used for boat painting were black and white and it was not until the twentieth century that the reds, greens, yellows and blues came into use.

Almost from the beginning, though, the boats of the Number Ones vied with each other to be the best decorated craft on the canal. Wherever a space could be found above water level, decoration appeared. The result was most beautiful and must have brought a dash of colour into some very harsh scenes at canal wharves and into the lives of the boatmen.

This is a museum replica of the decorated stern of a Narrow Boat. The horse's tail was probably hung on the rudderpost in memory of a dead horse

Obviously the parts most visible to other boatmen and the public were those most used for decoration: the 'cratch', cabin sides and fore ends of the boat being most prominent, as well as the cabin back. When motor boats came into use, they too were decorated but often not to the same extent as horse boats or the butty.

Inside the cabin

The boat cabin was the boatman's home and most families became justifiably proud of their cabins. To an outsider, the interior of a Narrow Boat cabin is an intriguing place. The entrance doors were usually decorated with roses and castles and a geometric pattern. The cabin itself, though small, was half filled with cupboards, a table, fold-away bed and stove. The insides of the cupboards generally were painted a dark colour, often blue or green, while the outsides, like nearly all the other outside surfaces, were finished in a light oak graining.

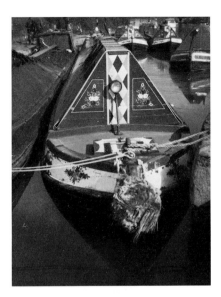

When a narrow boat approaches, the first part you see is the nearly triangular 'cratch', behind the headlamp. Here it has been painted with roses and diamond shapes

Interior of a narrow boat cabin, with a cooking range on the left and a shotgun with which to shoot rabbits for the pot. Between the cooker and the shotgun there is a folding table

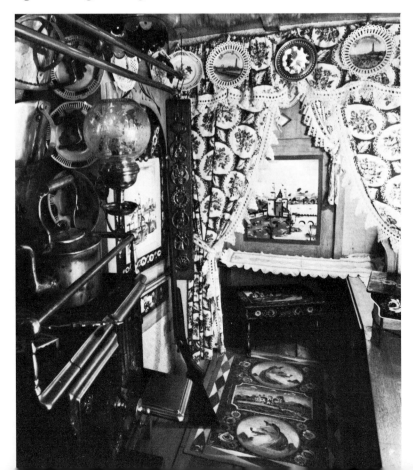

Sometimes the cupboard doors and the table cupboard had roses and castles on them. Around this decoration hung an array of ornaments: lace plates edged with brightly coloured ribbons, collected perhaps on holidays and handed from mother to daughter, mingled with lace work carefully crocheted by the boatwomen, often by the light of a paraffin lamp on a winter's evening. In this same light the highly polished brass knobs gleamed.

Teatime. The cupboard door folds down (left) to make a table. The underside of the table (right) is painted with a traditional design

Family photographs, or those of a favourite horse, found a place on the cabin walls.

Amidst all this, pride of place went to the Measham teapot, a type of brown pottery often inscribed with a verse or religious text. Like the lace plates, the teapot often remained in the same family for generations.

One piece of furniture found in nearly all cabins was the boatman's stool, a beautifully decorated article painted in traditional style. Originally this was both the bottom step into the cabin and its coal box. Although the cabin was small the main bed was often divided off from the rest of the cabin by a lace curtain. The whole effect of the inside of the cabin was one of a home well loved and cared for.

A Measham teapot

Left: Mr James, a retired boatman, giving a demonstration of traditional ropework. Right: the long thin piece is a 'swan's neck'

There was often shiny brass outside the cabin too. The stove chimney was detachable, since the boat had to pass through low tunnels, and the brass chain fastening it to the cabin roof was often hung with horse brasses. Many chimneys had three polished brass rings decorating the top. On the cabin roof stood the two water cans also decorated with a traditional design. On some boats even the mop was decorated.

Not every boatman lived in this way of course. Some boats had very little decoration and some of the single boatmen had neither time nor inclination to polish the brass. The majority of family boats, however, did try to keep up a high standard.

In addition to painting and brasswork, boat decoration also included some intricate ropework. One of the most attractive pieces was known as the *swan's neck*, found on the rudderpost. This was usually made by the boatman from a fine cotton line and was kept clean by regular scrubbing. Sometimes the swan's neck would be replaced by a horse's tail. Some people believe this was hung there in memory of a dead horse whose strength could be carried on in this way.

Clothing

A boatman's job involved him in heavy dirty work, opening greasy lock gates or trudging along a muddy towing path. His clothing, therefore, had to be hardwearing and able to stand up to all weathers. The boatman's trousers and waistcoat were normally made of mock moleskin or genuine corduroy, both very tough materials. He kept his trousers in place by a broad belt, made of leather or of a woven material, in which he could slip his windlass. The woven belt looked like a sash and was beautifully embroidered with a spider's web pattern. Braces often matched this design, though neither was really practical for everyday work. They were usually worn only on special occasions. Boatmen rarely wore shirts with collars, preferring instead a colourful neckerchief. Protection from rain and snow was vital and a boatman would wear a coat rather like a duffel coat, with a flat cap to protect his head.

Boatman's traditional 'spider's web' pattern belt with brass fittings and braces

The boatwoman too had to be kept warm, so she wore ankle length skirts covered by a wide apron. Her blouse was generally of a striped material worn with a shawl to keep her shoulders warm. The distinctive part of a boatlady's costume was her bonnet which became almost a symbol of the boatpeople's way of life.

As space on the boat was limited, the boatpeople's best clothes were often kept at a relative's house on the canal bank and brought out for special occasions.

A boatwoman of the 1890s, carrying a windlass or handle for operating lock paddles. Long skirt, shawl and heavy boots were worn by many working women at the time, but the bonnet was distinctive

A boat family dressed up for a formal photograph

Special occasions

Families worked such long hours that they had little time for visiting relatives or friends who worked on other boats. Often the nearest they might come to visiting would be when two families' boats passed in opposite directions.

Once a couple had begun courting, they obviously tried to see as much as possible of each other. Having tied up for the night a young boatman would get his bike off the boat, normally used for lockwheeling (riding on ahead of the boats to prepare the locks), and pedal up the towpath to see his girl, whom he may have passed during the day going in the other direction. Of course it was not every day that they passed and a week or more could go by before their two families' boats were close enough for another meeting.

A wedding party

Marriage

Eventually the couple might decide to get married and families and friends would get together for a celebration. The boat that the couple were to live on would be decorated with bunting and streamers and as many boat people as possible would try to attend.

The wedding itself generally took place at the parish church, close to where the boats were moored, and best clothes would be brought out for this occasion and for the reception, held in a local pub. This was a great opportunity for catching up on family news and gossip.

A courting couple

Just as today a bridegroom sometimes carries his bride into their home for the first time, a boatman would carry his bride on to the boat that was to become their home. The couple then set off for a honeymoon, sometimes for only a day; it all depended on how much work had to be done and whether they had their own boat.

Back at the public house the boatpeople enjoyed themselves, often into the early hours of the morning. But they would be up early the following morning, rushing to be the first through the locks. Some couples must have begun their first day of married life by starting work at 4 a.m.

Christenings and funerals

Another occasion to celebrate was the christening of a new baby and families and friends gathered for this.

The christening itself might be held at a local church or at an open air service on the canal bank, followed by great celebrations.

As a contrast, the death of a boatman was a very sad event in the life of the canal community. A boatman who had died away from home was often brought back on his own boat, usually bowhauled by friends or relations or pulled by a very steady horse. On this occasion the boat would be given right of way over all others on the canal. From the canal wharf to the church the coffin was borne by relatives or workmates, often with a large crowd of boatpeople behind.

Entertainment

Boatmen generally had little time for entertainment, but after a hard day's work they might call in at a canalside pub for a drink and a chat. In the pubs, boatmen enjoyed a good sing-song and many of them showed their skill at step-dancing and playing the melodian, accordion or banjo. On fine evenings they sometimes held impromptu concerts on the canal bank.

A boatman's accordion

A canal boat christening. Black bonnets were worn by many boatwomen after the death of Queen Victoria

The canal boats could not compete with the speed of the railways. This photograph was taken in 1936

8   Changes in a way of life

By 1848 almost eight thousand kilometres of railway were operating in the country and this transport system was quicker than the canals. Many canals were bought by railway companies. Some of them were closed while others were worked hard. Of those not bought, some closed through lack of trade, others fought the railway competition. But overall canal trade declined.

In the First and Second World Wars many boatmen joined the Armed Services and this left fewer men to crew the boats and maintain the canals. After each war, some men returned to the boats but others found better paid jobs away from the canals.

When canals were being built each engineer had his own ideas of sizes for the width of the canal and its locks. Some built locks wider and shorter than those of the narrow canals. This meant that goods travelling from a wide canal (such as the Sheffield and South Yorkshire Navigation) on to narrow canals had to change boats, maybe several times, as the wider boats of the wide canals would not fit the narrow locks. Similarly, Narrow Boats were too long for the locks of other canals. This made canal transport slower and more expensive, and drove customers away.

In the 1930s some efforts were made to win trade back to the canals. Locks on the Grand Union Canal north of Braunston towards Birmingham were widened to allow a motor boat and butty to fit in the lock side by side, as they normally travelled on wide stretches of canal. Also new boats were built for the newly formed Grand Union Canal Carrying Company. But trade continued to decline. Similarly, when the canals were nationalised in 1948, some attempts were made to improve trade but with little success.

The weather too aided the decline of canal carrying. In the winters of 1925 and 1947 nearly all canal traffic was stopped by several weeks of freezing weather and as a result more goods than ever were sent by rail or road. In the winter of 1962–3 another great freeze trapped the few boats left working and after this nearly all commercial carrying came to an end on the narrow canals.

This was the A1 road in 1955. It was not a dual carriageway, so the overtaking lorry is taking a risk. Once motorways were built, and other main roads improved, even the railways could not compete with the lorries—and canals lost what little trade they still had

As less and less goods were carried by canal, many boatmen had to leave the working boats. Some were glad to leave for better paid jobs. Others have stayed on the canals finding work as engineers or steerers with the ever increasing number of pleasure craft, or living in a boat on the canal and working at a job away from the canal during the day. Many have found it difficult to learn a new type of work and a new way of life. Their lack of education did not help them in this and many boatmen wanted a better education for their children.

Others have simply retired to a canalside cottage or boat moored on the canal, sometimes the boat in which they had spent their working life.

On the narrow canals, where commercial carrying has almost ceased, new pleasure cruisers have appeared, that are giving the canals a new lease of life.

On some wide canals, such as the Aire & Calder Navigation, commercial working continues where many tonnes of coal are carried, mainly to feed power stations.

Although the work was hard and often poorly paid, canal workers on the whole enjoyed their lives. Many of them have remarkable memories of their early lives and of amusing incidents during their time on the 'cut'.

A derelict canal—the end of the canal age for commercial carrying. But, surprisingly, this canal has been restored to full working order, since this photograph was taken in 1970, and is much used by pleasure cruisers

Places to visit

The Waterways Museum, Stoke Bruerne, Northants
The North-west Museum of Inland Navigation,
    Ellesmere Port, Cheshire
The Canal Museum, Dewsbury, Yorkshire

More books about canals

The story of our canals, Carolyn Hutchings (Ladybird)
Canals, Christine Vialls (A & C Black)
Britain's Inland Waterways, Roger Wickson
    (Methuen)
The following books are written for adults and give a
deeper perspective on various aspects of the canals.
The canals of Britain, D D Gladwin (Batsford)
Life afloat, Robert Wilson (Robert Wilson)
The Number Ones, Robert Wilson (Robert Wilson)
Narrow boats, L T C Rolt (Eyre Methuen)
The waterways of Britain, a social panorama,
    D D Gladwin (Batsford)
James Brindley, Harold Bode (Shire)
Canals in towns, Lewis Braithwaite (A & C Black)

Acknowledgements

The author and publishers are grateful to the following for
permission to reproduce illustrations:
British Waterways Board 2a, 7a & b, 9, 10b, 16a, 19a, 36, 41, 48,
49b, 50b, 51, 52b, 53b & c, 54a, 57, 59a & b, 62; Mary Evans
Picture Library 1, 4b, 6a, 16b, 22b, 43a; D D Gladwin 11, 13a, 15,
20a & b, 34b, 39, 43b, 44, 48a, 54b, 58a; Mansell Collection 2b, 4a,
5a, 5b, 14a, 18, 21, 22a, 24a & b, 58b; Hugh McKnight 3, 8b, 10a,
12a, 14b, 17, 19b, 26, 32, 33a & b, 34a, 37, 38, 39, 46b, 50a, 52a,
53a, 55, 56, cover; Radio Times Hulton Picture Library 13b, 23,
27a & b, 35a, 42, 47, 60, 61; Michael E Ware 8a, 12b, 25, 28, 29a &
b, 30, 31, 35b, 45, 46a; Waterways Museum, Stoke Bruerne, 22.

Index